'This edition produced for The Book People Ltd, Hall Wood Avenue, Haydock, St Helens, WA11 9UL
Published by the Penguin Group
Penguin Books Ltd, 80 Strand, London WC2R 0RL, England
Penguin Group (USA) Inc., 375 Hudson Street, New York, New York 10014, USA
Penguin Books (Australia) Ltd, 250 Camberwell Road, Camberwell, Victoria 3124, Australia.
(A division of Pearson Australia Group Pty Ltd)
Canada, India, New Zealand, South Africa
Published by BBC Children's Books, 2005
Text and design © Children's Character Books, 2005. Written by Stephen Cole
10 9 8 7 6 5 4 3 2 1
Printed in Great Britain by Clays Ltd, St Ives plc
ISBN 978-1-85613-161-2

DOCTOR·WHO
Quiz Book

CONTENTS

COULD YOU BE...
THE DOCTOR?

Have you ever dreamed of journeying through time and space? Do you long to fight monsters and right wrongs? How great is your appetite for danger? Not many people can do what the Doctor does. Take this test, tot up your scores, and measure your true Time Lord potential!

1. The TARDIS lands on an alien planet. The scanner shows nothing but sand and rock. Do you:

a) Go out and explore — you never know what you might find.

b) Take off again for somewhere more interesting.

c) Empty the TARDIS bins on the abandoned planet — you've been meaning to clean up for centuries.

2. You are walking along the street when a UFO flies overhead. Do you say:

a) Oh no, not another alien invasion!

b) Fantastic!

c) I'd better look it up in my UFO-spotters handbook to check if it's friendly or not!

3. You decide you would like a companion on your journeys through time and space. What qualities do you look for?

a) Someone brainy, brave and strong who can help you out of tight fixes.

b) Someone who will ask lots of questions and need rescuing a lot.

c) Someone who will help you see the universe in a different light.

4. Hostile aliens are roaming the streets of London wreaking destruction. Do you:

a) Advise the army how best to destroy the menace.

b) Confront their leader and warn them to leave — or else.

c) Set up a force field around London so the monsters can't take over anywhere else.

5. You accidentally find yourself at a conference of very important aliens from all over the galaxy. Do you:

a) Convince them that you have a right to be there so you can hang out for a while.

b) Point and giggle at all the funny species.

c) Take off immediately and leave them to it.

6. The TARDIS starts malfunctioning during flight. Do you:

a) Land immediately and check all systems, one by one.

b) Hit the console with a hammer.

c) Ignore it and hope for the best.

7. One of your companions steals rare gemstones from the king of an alien planet, hoping to sell them on Earth. Do you:

a) Take them straight back home and kick them off the TARDIS.

b) Insist they give the money they make to charity.

c) Make them put the gemstones back and warn them not to be greedy again.

8. You are very, very bored one night. Do you:

a) Speed-read a thousand books in one go — all that extra learning might be handy.

b) Add several thousand extra settings to your sonic screwdriver — it could help you get out of trouble in future.

c) Give the TARDIS a full overhaul — so it takes you exactly wherever and whenever you want to go.

9. While flying through space, a hideous alien creature appears inside the TARDIS and advances on your companion. Do you:

a) Rig up a device that will send it straight back where it came from.

b) Run from the control room with your companion and hope it goes away.

c) Try to communicate with it.

10. Which of the following do you find the most frightening:

a) A Slitheen.

b) A Dalek.

c) Your companion's mum joining you in the TARDIS.

COULD YOU BE THE DOCTOR?

Results:

1. a) 4 b) 1 c) 0
2. a) 1 b) 4 c) 2
3. a) 3 b) 1 c) 4
4. a) 2 b) 4 c) 1
5. a) 4 b) 0 c) 2
6. a) 1 b) 4 c) 1
7. a) 3 b) 1 c) 4
8. a) 3 b) 4 c) 0
9. a) 1 b) 0 c) 4
10. a) 3 b) 4 c) 8

How Did You Score?

36—44 You have true Time Lord potential, with an instinctive grasp of the dos and don'ts of time-space travel. One day the Doctor may regenerate into someone like you!

25—35 You are like the Doctor in many ways, but sometimes prone to panic and over-reacting. Take time out to assess each situation before acting — in case you regret what you do!

18—24 You have much to learn about travelling the universe, and your actions could cause disastrous consequences. If you hear of an imminent alien invasion, stand well back, leave it to the Doctor and pick up some tips!

17 or under You wouldn't know a TARDIS from a traffic light. Are you sure you're not a Slitheen in disguise, trying to mess up the universe at large? You should come with an intergalactic health warning!

WHEN PLASTIC ATTACKS!
TRUE OR FALSE?

The Earth was nearly invaded by living plastic...but were you paying attention? Say whether the statements below are true or false.

1. **The Nestene Consciousness can control all plastic.**
TRUE/FALSE

2. **Its servants are living plastic mannequins known as Autons.**
TRUE/FALSE

3. **The Nestene Consciousness was a kind creature that wanted to leave the Earth in peace.**
TRUE/FALSE

4. **It used Buckingham Palace as a transmitter.**
TRUE/FALSE

5. **Rose's boyfriend, Mickey, was snapped up by a living wheelie bin.**
TRUE/FALSE

6. An Auton stops working if you pull off its head.
TRUE/FALSE

7. Autons can disguise themselves as shop window dummies.
TRUE/FALSE

8. The Nestene Consciousness wants to turn the Earth into an enormous plastic factory.
TRUE/FALSE

9. Its world was destroyed in the Time War.
TRUE/FALSE

10. It infiltrated Earth's civilisation using warp shunt technology.
TRUE/FALSE

WHEN PLASTIC ATTACKS!

Answers:

1. True.	2. True.	3. False.	4. False.	5. True.
6. False.	7. True.	8. False.	9. True.	10. True.

Scores:

8-10 You're clearly an expert — no plastic's going to take you unawares.

5-7 Not a bad score, but you may be at risk if the Autons invade again.

0-4 If a vicious wheelie bin eats you up, don't come running to us!

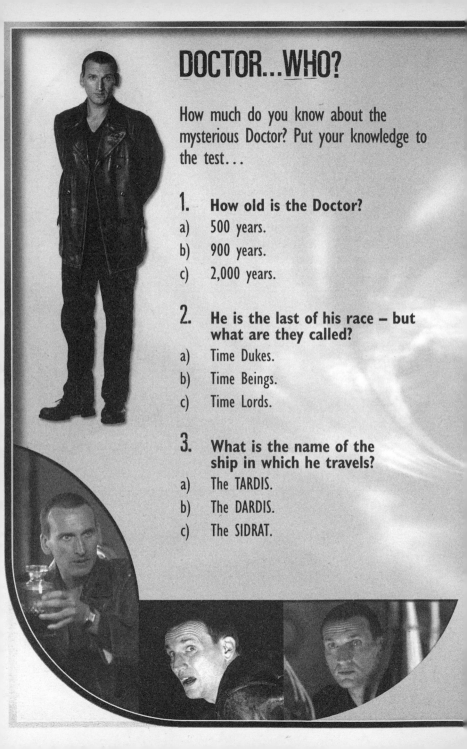

DOCTOR...WHO?

How much do you know about the mysterious Doctor? Put your knowledge to the test...

1. How old is the Doctor?
a) 500 years.
b) 900 years.
c) 2,000 years.

2. He is the last of his race – but what are they called?
a) Time Dukes.
b) Time Beings.
c) Time Lords.

3. What is the name of the ship in which he travels?
a) The TARDIS.
b) The DARDIS.
c) The SIDRAT.

4. To get past locked doors he uses:

a) A sonic spanner.

b) A sonic screwdriver.

c) A laser lance.

5. The Doctor fought in a terrible war, usually referred to as:

a) The Hyperspace War.

b) The TARDIS War.

c) The Time War.

6. How many hearts does the Doctor have?

a) One.

b) Two.

c) Three.

7. When the Doctor is excited he often shouts:

a) Splendid!

b) Cosmic!

c) Fantastic!

8. When the Doctor's body is damaged to the point of death, something extraordinary happens to save him...but what?

a) He regenerates into a new person.

b) He grows an extra heart.

c) He forms a chrysalis around himself to help him heal.

9. **How many languages does the Doctor speak?**

a) Five hundred.

b) Five thousand.

c) Five billion.

10. **When asked for official identification, what does the Doctor show?**

a) Slightly psychic ID, which shows people what they expect to see.

b) Universal Express card.

c) TARDIS driver's licence.

Answers:

1. b)	2. c)	3. a)	4. b)	5. c)
6. b)	7. c)	8. a)	9. c)	10. a)

Scores:

8-10 Fantastic! You know the Doctor like an old friend, and are clearly a loyal companion.

4-7 The Doctor remains a mystery to you but one you're keen to crack.

0-3 Wake up! There are adventures in time and space to be had — don't miss them!

THE END OF THE WORLD.
TRUE OR FALSE?

In five billion years the expanding sun will finally destroy the Earth. The Doctor and Rose witnessed its destruction…did you? Say whether the statements below are true or false.

1. **Alien VIPs gathered on a space station called Platform One to watch the Earth end.**
   TRUE/FALSE

2. **The stewards on board the space station were bright pink.**
   TRUE/FALSE

3. **The TARDIS was dragged off to a cloakroom and the Doctor was given a cloakroom ticket to get it back later.**
   TRUE/FALSE

4. **The full name of Cassandra, the last surviving human, is the Lady Cassandra O'Brien Dot Delta Seventeen.**
   TRUE/FALSE

5. The Earth was being kept alive by funding from English Heritage.
TRUE/FALSE

6. Cassandra released robotic slugs into the workings of the space station.
TRUE/FALSE

7. She had a transmat booster-feed hidden in an ostrich egg.
TRUE/FALSE

8. A super-advanced tree helped the Doctor save the space station.
TRUE/FALSE

9. Cassandra has had 708 cosmetic surgery operations.
TRUE/FALSE

10. Cassandra escaped justice by fleeing in a spaceship.
TRUE/FALSE

THE END OF THE WORLD.

Answers:

1. True.	2. False.	3. True.	4. True.	5. False.
6. False.	7. True.	8. True.	9. True.	10. False.

Scores

8-10 You know loads about the end of the world — you didn't stow away in the TARDIS, did you?

5-7 You weren't watching as closely as you could have been, but it's not the end of the world...

0-4 Would you even notice the world ending around you?!

ALL ABOUT ROSE.

Rose is the Doctor's top companion, and they are the closest of friends. But how well do you know her? Take the test and see if you're a best mate or a total state!

1. What is Rose's surname?
a) Wyler.
b) Tyler.
c) Smiler.

2. When Rose first met the Doctor she was working:
a) In a bank.
b) In a fast food restaurant.
c) In a department store.

3. What is the name of the place where Rose lives?
a) The Watt estate.
b) The Powell estate.
c) The Thyme estate.

4. **Rose's mum is called:**

a) Wendy.

b) Rachael.

c) Jackie.

5. **When the Doctor is held prisoner by the living plastic Autons, how does Rose save him?**

a) She shoots them with a space gun.

b) She sprays them with a fire extinguisher.

c) She knocks them into a vat of molten plastic.

6. **What happened to Rose's father?**

a) He was killed in a car accident.

b) He ran away with Rose's English teacher.

c) He was kidnapped by aliens.

7. **When did Rose first meet Captain Jack?**

a) In a spaceship orbiting Earth.

b) Hanging from a barrage balloon above war-torn London.

c) In a pink Cadillac.

8. **What is the name of Rose's former boyfriend?**

a) Ricky.

b) Dickie.

c) Mickey.

Scores:

6–8 You could be part of the Powell Estate posse — well done!

3–5 You know a bit about Rose, but clearly aren't too bothered.

0–2 What do you mean, "Rose who?"!

Answers:

1. b)	2. c)	3. b)	4. c)
5. c)	6. a)	7. b)	8. c)

ALL ABOUT ROSE.

22

ODD ONE OUT.

Look at the different groups of people, places and things below. In each case, which is the odd one out — and why?

1. Mickey, Rose, Jackie, Captain Jack.

2. Cassandra, The Face of Boe, Charles Dickens, The Moxx of Balhoon.

3. Mr Sneed, a Dalek, Gwyneth, the Gelth.

4. Cardiff, London, Platform One, Utah.

5. Adam Mitchell, a Slitheen egg, Harriet Jones, the head of an Auton.

6. Joe Green, Margaret Blaine, General Asquith, the Prime Minister.

ODD ONE OUT.

Answers:

1. Captain Jack — the others all come from 21st century London.
2. Charles Dickens — the others are all VIP guests on Platform One.
3. A Dalek — the others met their doom in Victorian Cardiff.
4. Platform One — the other landing sites are all on Earth.
5. Harriet Jones — the others have all travelled in the TARDIS.
6. The Prime Minister — the others were all used as Slitheen disguises.

Scores:

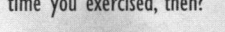

5–6   Excellent. Your powers of reasoning are almost as good as the Doctor's!

3–4   Pretty good going, but you know you can do better than this...

0–2   The mind is like a muscle — it needs exercising or it wastes away. When was the last time you exercised, then?

MONSTER MANIA!

Wherever the Doctor goes, there are normally monsters close by. He's an expert on aliens — how about you? Come out from behind the sofa and put your knowledge to the test…

1. **Where does an Auton conceal its deadly blaster?**

a) In its head.

b) In its leg.

c) In its wrist.

2. **What was the name of the 'lipstick and skin' creature who called herself the last surviving member of the human race?**

a) Cassandra.

b) Miranda.

c) Baccanda.

3. **The Gelth were creatures from another dimension who had an affinity with:**

a) Coal.

b) Cornflakes.

c) Gas.

4. **Which kind of animal did the Slitheen turn into an unlikely space pilot?**
a) A pig.
b) A cow.
c) A prawn.

5. **Where do the Reapers come from?**
a) The planet Reapos.
b) Inside the mind.
c) Outside time and space.

6. **Which of the following is the full title of the evil Jagrafess?**
a) The eternal Jagrafess of the Immense Jagulon Empire.
b) The mighty Jagrafess of the Holy Hadrojassic Maxarodenfoe.
c) The endless Jagrafess of the Jurassic Minidrivafriend.

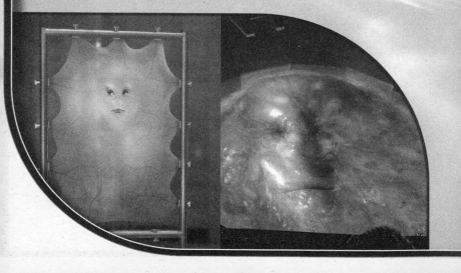

7. Which hideous creatures fought a time war against the Time Lords?

a) The Slitheen.

b) The Daleks.

c) The Autons.

Scores

6–7 You are a monster maniac - just make sure your brains don't mark you out as a target for alien invaders!

3–5 Not bad, but don't try to tackle monsters by yourself - you'll come off worst!

0–2 A monstrously bad mark - go and swot up on your alien races before it's too late!

Answers:

| 1. c) | 2. a) | 3. c) | 4. a) |
| 5. c) | 6. b) | 7. b) | |

MONSTER MANIA!

TARDIS TRAINED.

The TARDIS is a miracle of alien engineering. It makes doing the impossible seem easy. But how easy will you find this quiz about the Doctor's trusty time-and-spaceship?

1. **What does TARDIS stand for?**

a)   Trim And Regulated Driving In Space.

b)   Time And Related Disturbances In Space.

c)   Time And Relative Dimension In Space.

2. **What does the TARDIS look like from the outside?**

a)   A police telephone box.

b)   A police station.

c)   A big fridge.

3. **Which of these phrases best sums up the TARDIS?**

a)   Bigger on the outside than the inside.

b)   Bigger than the inside of the outside.

c)   Bigger on the inside than the outside.

4. **How does the TARDIS 'take off'?**

a) Its light flashes as it fades away.

b) Its rockets fire and it shoots up into the sky.

c) It spins around until it vanishes.

5. **What does the TARDIS key look like?**

a) A flat disc.

b) An ordinary key.

c) A metal tube that glows.

6. **What is housed beneath the TARDIS console?**

a) A drinks machine.

b) A nuclear reactor.

c) A living power source.

7. **How does the TARDIS locate the lair of the Nestene Consciousness?**

a) It uses an Auton head to trace the Nestene signal back to its source.

b) It scans London for alien energy emissions.

c) It follows an Auton who is heading back home.

8. When the Doctor tries to take Rose back to Naples in 1860, where does the TARDIS actually land?

a) Paris, 1865.

b) Cardiff, 1869.

c) Swansea, 1870.

9. What is the name of the device that would disguise the TARDIS wherever it lands – if it was working?

a) The chameleon circuit.

b) The invisibility shield.

c) The cloaking mechanism.

10. What fuel can be used to power the TARDIS?

a) Petrol.

b) Crushed hydrogen.

c) Radiation from a rift in time.

TARDIS TRAINED.

THE UNQUIET DEAD.
TRUE OR FALSE?

Almost 140 years ago, the world nearly ended, invaded by the Gelth. So...how is your history? Say whether the statements below are true or false.

1. **Going to Cardiff in 1869 was Rose's first trip through time.**
TRUE/FALSE

2. **Charles Dickens was reading from his novel *A Christmas Carol* on a theatre stage when a walking corpse interrupted him.**
TRUE/FALSE

3. **Rose was kidnapped from the theatre by an undertaker named Sneed.**
TRUE/FALSE

4. **The Doctor chased after them on a penny-farthing bicycle.**
TRUE/FALSE

5. **Sneed's servant girl, Gwyneth, was a powerful psychic medium who could read minds.**
TRUE/FALSE

6. The alien Gelth had the power to inhabit dead bodies.
TRUE/FALSE

7. The Gelth used Charles Dickens' mental power to propel themselves into our dimension.
TRUE/FALSE

8. The Doctor and Rose found themselves menaced by an army of zombies.
TRUE/FALSE

9. The Gelth were destroyed when Sneed's funeral parlour exploded.
TRUE/FALSE

10. Charles Dickens wrote a book based on his adventures with the Doctor.
TRUE/FALSE

Answers:

1. False.	2. True.	3. True.	4. False.	5. True.
6. True.	7. False.	8. True.	9. True.	10. False.

SCORES:

8–10 Your masterly mind is almost as great as the late Charles Dickens'!

5–7 You are a fair student with potential to do well — but you must try harder than this!

0–4 Your brain is so dead, a Gelth could take it over — watch out!

THE DREADED DALEKS.

The Doctor's greatest foes always have a few tricks up their sucker arms...you never know where or when they might strike! Test your knowledge of all things Dalek with this quiz...you never know when the information might come in handy!

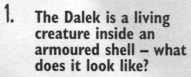

1. **The Dalek is a living creature inside an armoured shell – what does it look like?**

a) A pulsating crab with three eyes.

b) A one-eyed octopus with a big brain.

c) A giant yellow blob.

2. **Who is the leader of the Daleks?**

a) The Master.

b) The Emperor Dalek.

c) The Dalek of Daleks.

3. **How was the Doctor led to the Dalek being held prisoner in an underground museum?**

a) The Dalek sent a distress signal that drew the TARDIS off course.

b) He was hot on its trail and followed it to Earth.

c) He was invited to the museum's opening.

4. **What made-up name did Henry Van Statten give the Dalek he had captured?**

a) Metaltron.

b) Roboglider.

c) Bernard.

5. **What is a Dalek's most famous catchphrase?**

a) Annhilate!

b) Conquer the world!

c) Exterminate!

6. **How quickly can a Dalek calculate a thousand billion lock combinations?**

a) One second.

b) One minute.

c) One microsecond.

7. What does a Dalek do when faced with a flight of stairs?

a) It flies up them.

b) It panics.

c) It blows them up.

8. By what name is the Doctor known on the Dalek homeworld?

a) The traveller from beyond time.

b) The oncoming storm.

c) The Doctor.

THE DREADED DALEKS.

Answers:

1. b)	2. b)	3. a)	4. a)
5. c)	6. a)	7. a)	8. b)

Scores:

7–8   Your knowledge of the Daleks will serve you well should they invade the Earth again.

4–6   Should the Earth's Dalek experts get wiped out, the world will turn to you for help...so get ready!

0–3   It seems like your brain has already been exterminated! Go and have a lie down.

THE SLITHEEN.
TRUE OR FALSE?

How much do you know about these terrifying green meanies? Say whether the statements below are true or false.

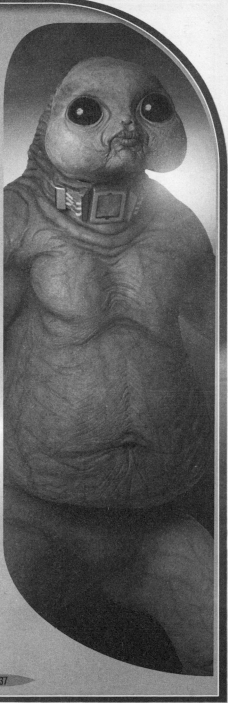

1. **The Slitheen come from the planet Slitheron.**
TRUE/FALSE

2. **A female Slitheen can fire poison darts from her claw.**
TRUE/FALSE

3. **Slitheen are made of slime.**
TRUE/FALSE

4. **The Slitheen planned to sell Earth to property developers.**
TRUE/FALSE

5. **'Slitheen' is only a surname, not the name of an alien race.**
TRUE/FALSE

6. Slitheen love to hunt.
TRUE/FALSE

7. Slitheen in disguise have zips in their foreheads.
TRUE/FALSE

8. Some Slitheen have personal teleport devices.
TRUE/FALSE

9. A Slitheen can be killed by concentrated vinegar.
TRUE/FALSE

10. A Slitheen feels the pain of another Slitheen.
TRUE/FALSE

THE SLITHEEN.

Answers:

1. False.	2. True.	3. False.	4. False.	5. True.
6. True.	7. True.	8. True.	9. True.	10. True.

Scores:

8-10 A superb score. You're not a Slitheen by any chance, are you?

5-7 Not bad, but you could still be caught out by a large person with wind problems and a zip in their forehead.

0-4 Let's hope that if the Slitheen come back, the defence of Earth doesn't depend on you!

TOUCHED BY THE TIME LORD.

This quiz focuses on the ordinary humans who have been drawn into the Doctor's hectic, dangerous life. How much do you know about them?

1. What is the name of the man who started his own website devoted to investigating the Doctor's life?

a) Rupert.

b) Mickey.

c) Clive.

2. What happened to him?

a) He was killed by a Dalek.

b) He was killed by a Slitheen.

c) He was killed by an Auton.

3. Who hacked into the Royal Navy's computer systems and fired a missile at 10 Downing Street with the Doctor's help?

a) Adam Mitchell.

b) Rose Tyler.

c) Mickey Smith.

4. **What childhood act confirmed that Adam Mitchell was a boy genius?**

a) He rewired a computer in thirty minutes flat.

b) He almost started World War Three when he was eight.

c) He beat a grandmaster at chess, five times in a row.

5. **What hideous creature nearly killed Jackie Tyler in her own flat?**

a) A Slitheen.

b) An Auton.

c) The Jagrafess.

6. **Which MP for Flydale North helped the Doctor and Rose fight the Slitheen?**

a) Millicent Smith.

b) Joe Green.

c) Harriet Jones.

7. **How does Rose keep in touch with her mum when she is travelling through time and space?**

a) By email.

b) She uses a modified mobile phone.

c) She uses a space communicator.

8. How did Jackie help Rose expose the power source within the TARDIS?

a) She found it in a locked room hidden in the centre of the ship.

b) She borrowed a lorry and used it with a tow rope to drag the console away.

c) She answered a series of logic puzzles to open the console.

CAPTAIN ON DECK!

He's the flashiest maverick in space — but does Jack's reputation go before him, or does the Captain leave you clueless? Find out by taking this test…

1. **What is Captain Jack's surname?**

a) Jones.

b) Ittin.

c) Harkness.

2. **Captain Jack used to be a special operative for a secret organisation. They called themselves:**

a) Time Agents.

b) Space Patrollers.

c) Time-Space Generals.

3. **Why did Captain Jack leave this organisation?**

a) He was bored with the lifestyle.

b) He was thrown out for breaking the rules.

c) He quit when his bosses stole two years of his memories.

4. **What did he become instead?**

a) A space-traffic policeman.

b) A con-artist.

c) A space smuggler.

5. **What type of gun was Captain Jack using when he first met the Doctor?**

a) A sonic blaster.

b) A glitter gun.

c) A demat gun.

6. **In Cardiff, while the Doctor ate dinner with a Slitheen and Rose talked with Mickey, what was Captain Jack doing?**

a) Dancing at a disco.

b) Converting an alien device into a fuel source for the TARDIS.

c) Watching videos.

7. **What type of ship was Captain Jack flying when he first met the Doctor?**

a) Chula.

b) Hula.

c) Hawksmith Vanguard 2000.

8. **When Captain Jack was killed by the Daleks, who brought him back to life?**

a) The Doctor.

b) The Emperor Dalek.

c) Rose.

CAPTAIN ON DECK!

Answers:

1. c)	2. a)	3. c)	4. b)
5. a)	6. b)	7. a)	8. c)

Scores:

7–8   Your knowledge of Captain Jack's life story is impressive. Were you ever his senior officer?

5–6   Not bad — you might just scrape into the Time Agent academy.

0–4   You're more of a regimental mascot than a captain — next time, try harder!

DALEK UNDERGROUND!
TRUE OR FALSE?

Thanks to the TARDIS, we know
that in just a few years from
now, a Dalek is due to break
out of a very special museum...
forewarned is forearmed — but
do you remember enough of
what you saw to tell true
statements from false?

1. **The alien museum was owned by billionaire
    Henry Van Statten.**
    TRUE/FALSE

2. **It is buried deep underground in Utah,
    North America.**
    TRUE/FALSE

3. **One whole floor has been converted into a prison
    for aliens.**
    TRUE/FALSE

4. **The Dalek prisoner was treated with kindness
    and respect.**
    TRUE/FALSE

5. When the Dalek saw the Doctor it tried to exterminate him.
TRUE/FALSE

6. The Dalek absorbed DNA from Adam Mitchell to start regenerating its damaged casing.
TRUE/FALSE

7. A Dalek can kill people with its sucker stick.
TRUE/FALSE

8. The Dalek became infected with human emotion.
TRUE/FALSE

9. Towards the end of its life, the Dalek wanted to feel the sunlight on its skin.
TRUE/FALSE

10. The Doctor shot it with a large alien gun.
TRUE/FALSE

DALEK UNDERGROUND!

Answers:

| 1. True. | 2. True. | 3. False. | 4. False. | 5. True. |
| 6. False. | 7. True. | 8. True. | 9. True. | 10. False. |

Scores:

8–10 You are a very observant Dalek expert!

5–7 You must be easily distracted — or perhaps you were hiding behind a cushion when you should have been watching!

0–4 EXTERMINATE!!!

THE SLITHEEN SCENE.

It's harder to rid yourself of a Slitheen than you might suppose... Like bad pennies, they keep turning up. But how much do you know about the Slitheen scene?

1. **What is the name of the Slitheen's home planet?**

a) Rexapelagoallabeedoshus.

b) Ruxalossophocalicawilberry.

c) Raxacoricofallapatorius.

2. **What was the full name of the head of the Slitheen family group on Earth?**

a) Jocrassa Fel Fotch Pasameer-Day Slitheen.

b) Bronco Fel Fotch Pasameer-Day Slitheen.

c) Narcissus Fel Fetch Pasameer-Night Slitheen.

3. **What are the Slitheen made of?**

a) Living calcium.

b) Living nitrogen.

c) Living potassium.

4. **Why do Slitheen burp and fart so much in their human disguises?**

a) To distract their enemies.

b) Because the Earth's atmosphere gives them wind.

c) The compression fields they use to shrink themselves create excess gas.

5. **Why did the Slitheen want to destroy the Earth?**

a) So they could sell chunks of it as scrap.

b) So they could sell chunks of it as fuel for spaceships.

c) So the people of Earth would never expand into space.

6. **How did Blon Fel Fotch survive the destruction of Downing Street?**

a) She teleported out of danger.

b) She burrowed a hole in the ground.

c) She hid inside a cabinet.

7. How can a female of the Slitheen species defend itself when in extreme danger?

a) Bite and scratch.

b) Manufacture a poison dart within her finger and exhale the excess poison through her lungs.

c) Hypnotise her enemy with her eyes and spray acid from her mouth.

8. What happens if a Slitheen child fails to carry out its first kill?

a) It is thrown out of the family.

b) It is fed to the venom grubs.

c) It is tortured for five days and then sent out to kill again.

WHAT ARE YOU LIKE?

Imagine if you got the chance to travel with the Doctor…just how would you cope with the dangerous situations that come with the TARDIS lifestyle? Take the test below and find out…

1. You find yourself on a busy space station where the Doctor suspects something is wrong. Do you:

a)   Stay close to him, wanting to be where the action is so you can fight evil together.

b)   Go off exploring on your own to see if you can find any clues.

c)   Pocket a few pieces of technology — they'll be worth a fortune back home!

2. You find a badly injured alien creature trapped inside a prison cell. It pleads for help. Do you:

a)   Enter the cell and try to help the alien, unable to stand by while it is in such pain.

b)   Look it up in your electronic alien database to see if its hostile — it might be in prison for a reason!

c)   Ignore it — the thing's probably dangerous.

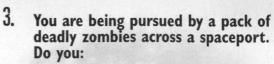

3. **You are being pursued by a pack of deadly zombies across a spaceport. Do you:**

a) Run for it, keeping an eye out for terrified innocent bystanders so you can help them.

b) Teleport out of danger, grab a sonic blaster and deal with the zombies single-handed.

c) Hide somewhere until they've gone, then sneak back to the TARDIS.

4. **Autons are invading London, attacking a shopping centre. What do you do?**

a) Phone your mum and check she's safely off the streets.

b) Track down the Nestene Consciousness and challenge it to a duel — if it loses, it calls off the invasion.

c) Wait till the Doctor defeats them, then help yourself to some living plastic — an invention like that's worth a fortune.

5. **You travel back fifty years in time on a sightseeing trip. Do you:**

a) Look up past relatives to see what they were really like in their youth.

b) Stock up on some trendy retro fashions and hope some action comes along soon.

c) Open a high-interest savings account — when you're back in your own time, it'll be worth loads.

6. **The Doctor takes you to an alien cocktail party. Do you:**

a) Check it out and marvel at the weirdness of it all.

b) Flirt with all the guests and party all night.

c) Ask the cleverest guests about science and technology, to see if you can use their ideas when you get back home.

7. **The Doctor is in trouble, held prisoner by two robots on a scaffold. Do you:**

a) Swing on a scaffolding rope, Tarzan-style, and knock the robots aside.

b) Blast the robots with a gun and carry the Doctor to safety on your back.

c) Distract the robots so they start to come after you — allowing the Doctor to overcome them.

8. **The Doctor takes you to the planet Woman Wept, where the beaches are a thousand miles across, and where frozen waves a hundred feet high rise up from the endless ocean. Do you:**

a) Walk with the Doctor at midnight, enjoying the moment, knowing it will stay with you for ever.

b) Hold a beach party and get out the barbecue.

c) Faint.

WHAT ARE YOU LIKE?

Mostly As

Your approach to time and space travel is a lot like Rose Tyler's. You realise you've been given an incredible opportunity, that it's a privilege to travel with the Doctor, and you're determined to get the most out of your time together. Whether you're fighting monsters on Mars or sightseeing on a far-distant moon, you realise that life is a great adventure and throw yourself into every new situation that comes along — while never forgetting that the universe doesn't revolve around you, and that the people around you may need your help. You're sensitive, caring and always ready to lay your life on the line for others.

Mostly Bs

You're a laid-back, devil-may-care kind of character, a bit like Captain Jack. You live for adventure, dashing and smashing your way through life with a lot of laughs and a great deal of style. For you, space is a playground and you're determined to enjoy yourself. But when unpleasant aliens are about and people's lives are in danger, the playing around ends — you make it your mission to save the day, often with the help of handy high-tech gadgets (that's what they're there for, right?). But remember, there's a serious side to the universe, and one day you may have to grow up a little and face up to that... until then, party on!

Mostly Cs

You have a lot in common with sneaky Adam Mitchell. While Rose sees time travel as a way of making a difference, and Captain Jack breezes through life being outrageous, you are always thinking of what the universe can do for you. You are not brave, and have a strong instinct for self-preservation — after all, it would be terrible if someone as clever as you was killed while sticking your neck out for somebody else. You have a genuine interest in the culture and science of other planets, but at the back of your mind you're always imagining how you might profit from it back on Earth. If you want to stay travelling with the Doctor, you must learn to put others first now and then.

THE LONG GAME.
TRUE OR FALSE?

Travel to Satellite Five in the far future,
where the broadcast news is far more
important than anyone can guess. Say true
or false to these statements about the story,
and hope that no one is influencing your
answers...

1. **The TARDIS takes the Doctor, Rose
   and Adam to the year 200,000.**
   TRUE/FALSE

2. **Everyone on Satellite Five uses
   beads and necklaces instead
   of money.**
   TRUE/FALSE

3. **All the news from every planet is collected
   in a rush of data called an info-spike.**
   TRUE/FALSE

4. **News-gatherers have
   little doorways in their
   heads that open up to
   receive the info-spike.**
   TRUE/FALSE

5. When workers are 'promoted' they are secretly killed.
TRUE/FALSE

6. The Editor is a kindly figure who looks after everyone aboard Satellite Five.
TRUE/FALSE

7. He is the ruling intelligence of Satellite Five.
TRUE/FALSE

8. The Jagrafess is a hideous monster that lives on Floor 500.
TRUE/FALSE

9. If the Jagrafess overheats, it explodes very messily.
TRUE/FALSE

10. The Editor escapes the destruction of Floor 500 by rushing to the lift.
TRUE/FALSE

SCORES:

7–10 You have a lively and inquiring mind — unlike most humans on board Satellite Five!

4–6 You need to ask more questions and pay attention to the answers — you've got a good mind, use it or lose it!

0–3 No point putting an info-spike in your head — there's no brain inside! Pay more attention in future (and in the past for that matter...).

Answers:

1. True.	2. False.	3. True.	4. True.	5. True.
6. False.	7. False.	8. True.	9. True.	10. False.

FUTURE HISTORY.

The Doctor's travels have given
us a precious peek into the
future of the human race...but
how much can you remember
from his excursions into the
years yet to come?

1. **What, according to
the Doctor, will future
Prime Minister Harriet
Jones one day be the
architect of?**

a) Britain's Golden Age.

b) Britain's Dreadful Decade.

c) Britain's Silver Empire.

2. **In the year 200,000, what was the name of the space
station broadcasting the news?**

a) Platform One.

b) Satellite Five.

c) News Station 247365.

3. **By what name is it known a hundred years later,
when the Doctor returns?**

a) Satellite Seven.

b) The Game Station.

c) Game-show World.

4. **The year 12,005 AD falls in which period of human history?**

a) The Second Roman Empire.

b) The Third French Quango.

c) The Rootless Era of Forest-Dwellers.

5. **What is the precise year in which the Earth is destroyed by the Sun?**

a) Five zillion AD.

b) Five-point-five-slash-apple-slash-twenty-six.

c) Fourteen billion, seventeen million, two thousand and three.

6. **In what year did Adam Mitchell board the TARDIS?**

a) 2012.

b) 2112.

c) 3000.

7. **What happens to evicted housemates on Big Brother in the year 200,100?**

a) They are executed.

b) They are put in prison.

c) They are secretly teleported away and turned into Daleks.

8. **How did a Dalek from the far future end up on 21st century Earth?**

a) It fell through time.

b) It rode there in a time machine.

c) It stowed away in the TARDIS.

FUTURE HISTORY.

Answers:

1. a)	2. b)	3. b)	4. a)
5. b)	6. a)	7. c)	8. a)

Scores:

6–8   Well done! You know your history all right — even the stuff that hasn't happened yet!

3–5   Not bad, but you've got a lot more studying to do if you want to be a future historian.

0–2   Oh dear — your future as a Doctor Who mastermind isn't looking too bright with a score like this! But remember, the future can be changed...it's up to you!

REAPER ALERT!
TRUE OR FALSE?

If you mess about with time, terrible things can happen. Say whether the statements below are true or false.

1. **Rose's dad died in a hit-and-run accident in 1987.**
   TRUE/FALSE

2. **Rose secretly wants to save her dad from being killed.**
   TRUE/FALSE

3. **When Rose saves her dad, it has no consequences for the planet Earth.**
   TRUE/FALSE

4. **The TARDIS is pulled through a wound in time and ceases to exist in our world.**
   TRUE/FALSE

5. **The Reapers are predators from outside this universe.**
   TRUE/FALSE

6. **Everyone they catch is locked up in a big, dark room.**
   TRUE/FALSE

7. **The Doctor leads people to the safety of a church.**
TRUE/FALSE

8. **They wait inside until the Reapers give up and go home.**
TRUE/FALSE

9. **The Doctor is stronger than the Reapers, and survives their attack on him.**
TRUE/FALSE

10. **Rose's dad sacrifices his life to put history back on course.**
TRUE/FALSE

...the answers! You should know what can happen when you try to change history...

Whatever you do, don't try to go back in time and take the quiz again now you know

0–4

Good going, but if you pay more attention you will reap bigger rewards!

5–7

You have a mind as sharp as a Reaper's claws — well done!

8–10

Scores:

6. False.	7. True.	8. False.	9. False.	10. True.
1. True.	2. True.	3. False.	4. True.	5. True.

Answers:

REAPER ALERT!

TAKING THE MICKEY!

Mickey Smith is Rose's ex-boyfriend, and a reluctant ally in the Doctor's fight against alien aggressors. How well do you know him?

1. **The Doctor often pretends to get Mickey's name wrong. What does he call him?**

a) Sicky.

b) Ricky.

c) Nigel.

2. **What kind of car does Mickey drive?**

a) A blue BMW.

b) A clapped-out green Ford Escort.

c) A yellow VW Beetle.

3. **Why did the Nestene Consciousness make a living plastic replica of Mickey?**

a) To test a new plastic process.

b) So it could use it to find out what Rose knew about the Doctor.

c) Because Mickey knew too much about its plans.

4. **Where was the real Mickey held prisoner while his replica was at large?**

a) In the Nestene Consciousness's lair beneath the London Eye.

b) In his flat.

c) In a plastic spaceship orbiting the Earth.

5. **Why was Mickey taken in for questioning by the police when Rose first joined the Doctor?**

a) She was gone a year and they thought he'd murdered her.

b) They wanted to know about the Doctor.

c) They thought he had committed a robbery.

6. **Why did Mickey choose not to go with the Doctor and Rose on their adventures?**

a) The Doctor is too rude to him.

b) He knows he can't handle their dangerous lifestyle.

c) His passport is not valid.

7. **Who did Mickey start going out with when he broke up with Rose?**

a) A movie actress.

b) A model.

c) Trisha Delaney from the shop.

8. **What alien creature does Mickey help the Doctor catch along with Rose and Captain Jack?**

a) A Dalek.

b) A Reaper.

c) Blon Fel Fotch Pasameer-Day Slitheen.

TAKING THE MICKEY!

THE EMPTY CHILD.
TRUE OR FALSE?

When the Doctor and Rose pitched up in London during the Second World War, a terrifying adventure lay ahead... If you shared it with them, you should be able to sort the true statements from the false!

1. The **TARDIS** followed an unidentified alien capsule to Earth with no trouble at all.
   TRUE/FALSE

2. Rose found herself dangling from a barrage balloon high above London.
   TRUE/FALSE

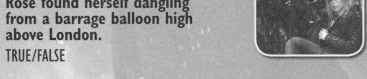

3. She was rescued by the Doctor.
   TRUE/FALSE

4. The Doctor was taken to an eerie hospital by Dr Constantine.
   TRUE/FALSE

5. All the patients had the same injuries and wore gas masks.
   TRUE/FALSE

6. **They were being controlled by a strange, scary child looking for his mum.**
TRUE/FALSE

7. **The child had been brought back from the dead by alien nanogenes.**
TRUE/FALSE

8. **The Doctor couldn't find the child's mother.**
TRUE/FALSE

9. **The Doctor couldn't save everyone and turn them back to normal.**
TRUE/FALSE

10. **Captain Jack decided not to join the Doctor and Rose on their travels.**
TRUE/FALSE

THE EMPTY CHILD.

Answers:

1. False.	2. True.	3. False.	4. True.	5. True.
6. True.	7. True.	8. False.	9. False.	10. False.

Scores:

8—10 Your skills of recall are remarkable.

5—7 Not bad — though you could use a few nanogenes to rebuild your brain cells!

0—4 Never mind the Empty Child — you have the Empty Head!

USEFUL THINGS TO HAVE...

The Doctor is never short of ingenious solutions to terrifying problems, Captain Jack has a useful gadget for every emergency, and alien creatures excel at using lethal devices. But at the end of the day, a quick mind is the most useful thing to own of all — test out yours right now!

1. **What does the Doctor use to destroy the Nestene Consciousness?**

a) A bottle of paint stripper.

b) A sonic blaster.

c) A tube of anti-plastic.

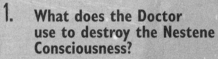

2. **What does Captain Jack use to heal Rose's cut hands in 1941?**

a) Antiseptic cream.

b) Sub-atomic healing robots.

c) Chula cough drops.

3. The cheapest way to interface with the computers on Satellite Five is a Type One Head-chip inserted into the back of the skull. How much does it cost?

a) One hundred credits.

b) One credit.

c) One million credits.

4. In war-torn London, the Doctor instructs Rose to use the sonic screwdriver on setting 2,428-D. What does this do?

a) Ignites marsh gas.

b) Sends a distress signal.

c) Re-attaches cut barbed wire.

5. What is special about Captain Jack's handcuffs, as worn by Blon the Slitheen?

a) They dig into her wrists if she tries to escape.

b) They can be magnetised, pinning her to any metal surface.

c) They zap the prisoner with ten thousand volts if she tries to escape.

6. How does Captain Jack keep his spaceship hidden from public view?

a) He parks it underground.

b) It has a cloaking device.

c) It is coated in chameleon skins.

7. What does the Doctor entrust to Mickey at the end of the first Slitheen attack on Earth?

a) A special computer virus that will wipe out all trace of the Doctor from the Internet.

b) A special Slitheen detector.

c) A spare TARDIS key.

8. Blon planned to escape Earth using a 'pan-dimensional surfboard' – but what, according to Captain Jack, is its full technical name?

a) A tribophysical waveform macro-kinetic extrapolator.

b) A super-advanced motion-field wave-rider.

c) An enhanced shockwave-energy mass-extractor.

9. What happened when this device was connected to the TARDIS console during a Dalek attack?

a) Nothing.

b) It generated a powerful force field.

c) It turned the TARDIS invisible.

10. How does the 'vomit-o-matic' work on Satellite Five?

a) If you're sick, microscopic cleaning robots clear up the mess.

b) If you're sick, nano-termites in the lining of the throat freeze it to avoid mess.

c) It allows you to fake sickness so you can skive off work or school.

USEFUL THINGS TO HAVE...

Answers:

1. c)	2. b)	3. a)	4. c)	5. c)
6. b)	7. a)	8. a)	9. b)	10. b)

Scores:

8–10   You know your neutron flow from your proton exchange all right! A score worthy of a true mad scientist!

4–7   Your knowledge of weird science is quite impressive, but there's scope for improvement.

0–3   Have you sold your brain to medical science? If so, run, before they want their money back!

ODD ONE OUT.

In each of the groupings below there is an odd one out...
Seek it out and exterminate it!

1. The Anne Droid, a Slitheen, Trin-E, Zu-Zana.

2. The Emperor Dalek, one of Cassandra's sabotage spiders, the
   Nestene Consciousness, the Jagrafess.

3. Cassandra, The Doctor, Captain Jack, Van Statten's Dalek.

4. Clive in a shopping centre, Lynda on Satellite Five, Suki on
   Satellite Five, Harriet Jones in 10 Downing Street.

5. A bicycle pump, a seat, a kitchen sink, a hammer.

6. Gwyneth, Rose's dad, Jabe the tree, Dr Constantine.

ODD ONE OUT.

Answers:

1. A Slitheen — the others are deadly robot hosts on the game station.
2. The sabotage spider — the others are all monsters who rule.
3. Captain Jack — the others all believe they are the last of their kind.
4. Harriet Jones — the others were killed by alien monsters.
5. The kitchen sink — the others can all be found in the TARDIS control room.
6. Dr Constantine — the others all sacrificed themselves to save the lives of others.

Scores:

6–8 A fantastic score in a very hard quiz! You are a true expert on the Doctor and his adventures.

4–5 Still a pretty impressive result. You are a bright spark, and are bound to get brighter still.

2–3 Not bad — at least there's no danger of Henry Van Statten asking you to join his underground museum staff!

0–1 Oops. Better luck next time — meanwhile, give that brain cell of yours a good rest!

BOOM TOWN.
TRUE OR FALSE?

The Doctor wasn't expecting to run into the Slitheen again after the last time they tangled — but life is full of surprises. Can you say whether the statements below are true or false?

1. **The Doctor took the TARDIS to a rift in space and time in Cardiff for refuelling.**
   TRUE/FALSE

2. **He found that one of the Slitheen family, Blon Fel Fotch, had survived the explosion in Downing Street.**
   TRUE/FALSE

3. **Blon Fel Fotch had set up a hamburger stand in the Millennium Centre Square.**
   TRUE/FALSE

4. **When she was found by the Doctor, she gave up without a struggle.**
   TRUE/FALSE

5. **She had planned to escape Earth by setting off a nuclear reactor on top of the rift and riding the shockwave to a different planet.**
   TRUE/FALSE

6. The Doctor planned to take her to a space prison where she would be locked up for 100 years.

TRUE/FALSE

7. The Doctor and the Slitheen went out for dinner together.

TRUE/FALSE

8. Blon Fel Fotch didn't try to kill him once.

TRUE/FALSE

9. She sneakily used a high-tech gadget to open the rift in an attempt to escape.

TRUE/FALSE

10. The power at the heart of the TARDIS reversed her time-stream, turning her back into an egg.

TRUE/FALSE

BOOM TOWN.

Answers:

1. True.	2. True.	3. False.	4. False.	5. True.
6. False.	7. True.	8. False.	9. True.	10. True.

Scores:

8–10 An explosively good score — almost good enough to open a rift in time and space!

5–7 A fairly impressive result — good enough to start a medium-sized explosive reaction.

0–4 Fairly feeble — you might just ignite a paper bag with a score like that. Better luck next time!

FOLLOW THE BIG BAD WOLF.

Wherever the Doctor and Rose go, the words BAD WOLF seem to crop up. Different times, different places...like it's written across the universe. But just where exactly did all those references crop up...?

1. **Where was the phrase first heard?**
a) In Victorian Cardiff.
b) On Platform One.
c) In a tent in Naples.

2. **On Platform One, who spoke of a 'bad wolf scenario' taking place?**
a) The Face of Boe.
b) The Steward.
c) Jolco and Jolco.

3. **Who said they could see the big, bad wolf when the Gelth tried to cross into our dimension?**
a) Gwyneth, the servant girl.
b) Sneed, the undertaker.
c) Charles Dickens, the author.

4. The words 'Bad Wolf' were seen scrawled as graffiti in the Doctor's next adventure – but where?

a) In a hospital.

b) On the TARDIS.

c) On the door of 10 Downing Street.

5. 'Bad Wolf One' was the call-sign for which vehicle?

a) The Steward's shuttle on Platform One.

b) Henry Van Statten's helicopter.

c) A barrage balloon in 1940s London.

6. What was showing on Badwolf TV on Satellite Five?

a) Coverage of a war on Vortis.

b) Coverage of a famine on Earth.

c) Coverage of the Face of Boe expecting baby Boemina.

7. Where did the phrase appear when the TARDIS landed in 1987?

a) On a wedding invitation.

b) Nowhere.

c) In graffiti.

8. What was written on the German bomb Captain Jack took into his spaceship?

a) Bad Wolf.

b) Schlechter Wolf.

c) Achtung Wolf!

9. 'Blaidd Drwg' means 'Bad Wolf' in Welsh. It was also the name of:

a) The restaurant in Cardiff where the Doctor and a Slitheen had dinner.

b) The hotel in Cardiff where Mickey was staying.

c) The unstable nuclear power station in Cardiff.

10. Who runs the Game Station?

a) The Bad Wolf Corporation.

b) The Bad Wolf Syndicate.

c) The Bad Wolf Gaming Programme.

11. When do the Doctor and Rose first realise the words BAD WOLF are appearing wherever they go?

a) In Van Statten's museum.

b) In Cardiff Town Hall.

c) In a tent in Naples.

12. Who spread the words 'Bad Wolf' through the universe as a kind of trail for the TARDIS to follow?

a) The Daleks.

b) The Editor.

c) Rose.

FOLLOW THE BIG BAD WOLF.

Answers:

1. b)	2. a)	3. a)	4. b)	5. b)
6. c)	7. b)	8. b)	9. c)	10. a)
11. b)	12. c)			

Scores:

10–12 You clearly love a good mystery — not much gets past you!

6–9 You have an enquiring mind but to keep it sharp you must keep your eyes open.

3–5 You will get more out of life if you pay attention to the little details as well as the big ones!

0–2 Better watch out — with a score like that, the Big Bad Wolf will be coming for YOU!

QUALITY QUOTATIONS.

Who first said the following memorable words? Clear out your ears and see if any of these quality quotations stick in your mind…

1. "I can feel it – the turn of the Earth… The ground beneath our feet is spinning at a thousand miles an hour…"

a) Jackie.

b) The Doctor.

c) A Dalek.

2. "You're just skin, Cassandra. Lipstick and skin!"

a) Jabe.

b) The Moxx of Balhoon.

c) Rose.

3. "This is not life. This is sickness. I shall not be like you! Order my destruction! Obey! Obey! Obey!"

a) The Doctor.

b) Henry Van Statten.

c) A Dalek.

4. **"D'you think it's cheap, looking like this? Flatness costs a fortune."**
a) Cassandra.
b) Blon Fel Fotch.
c) The Editor.

5. **"The Doctor is a legend, woven through history. When disaster comes, he is there. He brings the storm in his wake and he has one constant companion...death!"**
a) Captain Jack.
b) Mickey.
c) Clive.

6. **"Let me tell you something about the human race. You put a mysterious blue box slap bang in the middle of town – what do they do? Walk past it."**
a) The Editor.
b) The Doctor.
c) Harriet Jones.

7. **"See you in hell!"**
a) Captain Jack.
b) Jabe.
c) The Editor.

8. "EXTERMINATE!"

a) The Moxx of Balhoon.

b) The Nestene Consicousness.

c) The Daleks.

THE PARTING OF THE WAYS.
TRUE OR FALSE?

In the gripping conclusion of the Ninth Doctor's adventures, nothing was safe and there was nowhere to hide. Say if the statements below are true or false — if you dare!

1. **The Doctor, Rose and Captain Jack were all abducted from the TARDIS and placed in futuristic game shows.**
   TRUE/FALSE

2. **The Doctor found himself playing Can't Cook, Won't Cook.**
   TRUE/FALSE

3. **He soon realized that he and his companions were back on Platform One, only further in the future.**
   TRUE/FALSE

4. **The Doctor learned that the Daleks were the power behind all the game shows.**
   TRUE/FALSE

5. **The Daleks captured Rose to ensure the Doctor would not interfere with their plans.**
   TRUE/FALSE

6. They planned to invade Mars and turn all Martians into Daleks.
TRUE/FALSE

7. The Doctor rescued Rose and sent her back to Earth in the TARDIS, alone, where she would be safe.
TRUE/FALSE

8. Rose used the TARDIS instruction manual to fly it back to the Doctor.
TRUE/FALSE

9. Rose, possessed by the Time Vortex, destroys the Daleks – then the Doctor takes the vortex into himself before it can harm her.
TRUE/FALSE

10. The Doctor suffers no ill-effects as a result of his bravery...
TRUE/FALSE

THE PARTING OF THE WAYS.

Answers:

| 1. True. | 2. False. | 3. False. | 4. True. | 5. True. |
| 6. False. | 7. True. | 8. False. | 9. True. | 10. False. |

Scores:

8–10   You were clearly with the Doctor right to the end – a loyal and knowledgeable fan!

5–7   Your memory seems a bit hazy – you're probably still suffering from shell-shock!

0–4   Do you actually have a memory?

THE MEGA CHALLENGE.

This final quiz is designed to test your detailed knowledge of Doctor Who. It's longer, harder and more challenging than the others...and it will separate the Doctor's casual acquaintances from his loyal companions. If you want to make it even tougher, set yourself a three-minute time limit for all 30 questions!

Good luck. Are you ready? Then...GO!

1. **What did the Doctor say when he first met Rose Tyler?**

a) "Hello, I'm the Doctor."

b) "Look out behind you!"

c) "Run!"

2. **The stuffed arm of which old enemy of the Doctor was found mounted in Henry Van Statten's alien museum?**

a) A Cyberman.

b) The Editor.

c) A Slitheen.

3. Why couldn't the Slitheen use the body of the Prime Minister as one of their disguises?

a) He was too slim for them to fit inside.

b) He smelled too much.

c) His body was too badly damaged when they killed him.

4. What is the name given to the age in which Satellite Five operates?

a) The Second Great Human Dynasty.

b) The Fourth Great and Bountiful Human Empire.

c) The Third Imperial Human Space Network.

5. What password does Mickey use repeatedly when hacking into secure military websites?

a) Blue Box.

b) Buffalo.

c) Bible.

6. What were the names of the TV presenter robots who wanted to change Captain Jack's image on Satellite Five?

a) Ethel and Beryl.

b) Trin-E and Zu-Zana.

c) Zog and Zug.

7. What piece of old-fashioned technology does Cassandra, the last surviving human being, mistake for an iPod?

a) A jukebox.

b) A fridge.

c) A vacuum cleaner.

8. Whereabouts on Earth did the Dalek crash-land before it was acquired by Henry Van Statten?

a) The Ascension Islands.

b) Russia.

c) Spain.

9. Why does everyone seem to speak English on the planets the Doctor and Rose visit?

a) Because they are English.

b) Because the TARDIS's telepathic field gets into Rose's head and translates.

c) Because the Doctor gives his friends special translating hearing aids.

10. Cassandra's father was a Texan, but where did her mother come from?

a) The Arctic desert.

b) The Sahara ice caps.

c) Luton.

11. **What sort of star will the Sun turn into when it expands?**

a) A red dwarf.

b) A white midget.

c) A red giant.

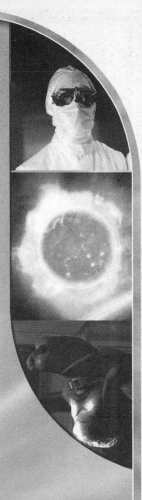

12. **How are criminals executed on the Slitheen's planet?**

a) Hanged, drawn and quartered.

b) Shot by a firing squad.

c) Boiled alive in acid.

13. **How many times was Mickey taken in for questioning by the police about Rose's disappearance?**

a) Three times.

b) Five times.

c) Four times.

14. **What does the Satellite Five snack 'zaffic' taste like?**

a) A beef flavoured slush-puppy.

b) A sweet-and-sour sticky bun.

c) Chicken curry with lemons.

15. **What was the name of the military doctor who examined the Slitheen's pig pilot?**

a) Dr Ghoulash.

b) Dr Sato.

c) Dr Hoo.

16. What did Rose mistake the Autons for when they first attacked her?

a) Students.

b) Security guards.

c) A street gang.

17. On Platform One, what colour was the plumber Rose met?

a) Purple.

b) Yellow.

c) Blue.

18. According to Henry Van Statten, where did the technology for Broadband come from?

a) The crashed UFO at Roswell.

b) An alien computer.

c) The Dalek.

19. What is the name of Rose's dad?

a) Paul.

b) Russell.

c) Pete.

20. To which anarchist organisation did Satellite Five worker Suki Cantrell belong?

a) The Red Fist.

b) The Freedom Foundation.

c) The New Justice Alliance.

21. What hardly-human creature was in charge of programming on the Game Station?

a) The Controller.

b) The Director.

c) The Game Vendor.

22. In the time of the Game Station, what storm has been raging on Earth for the last twenty years?

a) The Pacific Whirlpool.

b) The Great Atlantic Smog Storm.

c) The Towering Torquay Tornado.

23. What was the name of the department store where Rose used to work?

a) Henrik's.

b) Ibsen's.

c) Finch's.

24. What does Trin-E and Zu-Zana's defabricator do?

a) Measures how truthful you are being.

b) Removes clothing completely.

c) Removes stains from clothing.

25. What does a Slitheen egg resemble?

a) A small, blue cube.

b) A round, black ball.

c) A smooth oval with dreadlocks!

26. What does the Emperor Dalek believe himself to be?

a) The god of the Daleks.

b) The ruler of the whole universe.

c) A lumberjack.

27. What did Rose ask Mickey to bring to Cardiff for her?

a) Some magazines.

b) Her passport.

c) Her favourite shoes.

28. When the Doctor and Rose are trapped in 1987, which of the following helps bring the TARDIS back into existence?

a) A church pew.

b) Jackie's big hairdo.

c) A mobile phone battery.

29. What is written along the top of the TARDIS?

a) Police Public Call Box.

b) Police Telephone Box.

c) Police Free For Public.

30. How many legs do Cassandra's sabotage spiders have?

a) Eight.

b) Six.

c) Four.

POLICE PUBLIC CALL BOX

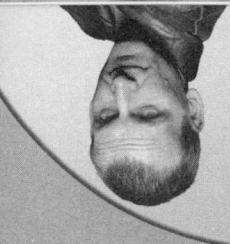

THE MEGA CHALLENGE

Answers:

1. c)	2. c)
3. a)	4. b)
5. b)	6. b)
7. a)	8. a)
9. b)	10. a)
11. c)	12. c)
13. b)	14. a)
15. b)	16. a)
17. c)	18. a)
19. c)	20. b)
21. a)	22. b)
23.a)	24. b)
25. c)	26. a)
27. b)	28. c)
29. a)	30. c)

Scores:

26–30 A truly impressive demonstration of Doctorish knowledge. Have you cheated and had an info-spike installed in your head?

22–25 Your remarkable powers of memory recall mark you out from the crowd. You can be proud of this result.

17–21 A solid foundation upon which to build your knowledge of the Doctor and his universe.

10–16 You were guessing a lot of these questions, weren't you?

5–9 There must be a malfunctioning data chip in your head!

0–4 Report to Floor 16, Medical, at once!